Jerom

"Gho

Ghost Town Stories
&
Wicked Legends

By
Peggy Hicks

Editing and Cover Design by
Dennis Andrews

ISBN-13: 978-0692289174

Published by: Peggy Hicks
Distributed by: Arizona Discoveries
317 Main Street
Jerome, Arizona 86331
928-301-3671

Ghost Town Stories & Wicked Legends blends the past with the present, and historical places with fictional characters in a collection of 13 short, allegorical tales creating unforgettable ghost stories.

Ghost Stories and Wicked Legends
By Peggy Hicks

Photos and illustrations are from the author's personal collection.

Introduction

Jerome, Arizona is located in Central Arizona, approximately 100 miles north of Phoenix and 45 miles southwest of Flagstaff on State Highway 89A. Today, it is a tourist destination and artist community of about 400 residents. This, however, has not always been the case.

In the early twenties this prosperous copper mining town's population exceeded 15,000. The town was packed with hard rock miners, crooked bureaucrats, bootleggers, dope peddlers, and prostitutes. It was so filled with vice that the New York Sun's newspaper dubbed it the **"Wickedest town in the West."**

With all this dangerous living, tragic deaths were sure to follow. People died in mining accidents, gunfights, opium overdoses and alcoholism along with a number of other unnatural events.

With its violent past, it comes as no surprise that this **"Ghost City"** on the hill is rumored to be filled with wandering spirits.

Dedicated

To those who believe
that ghosts exist...
and to those who don't want to
believe that ghosts exist.

Table of Contents

8. An Opium Addicted Feline "China Doll"
   (English Kitchen)

9. New Year's Eve at the Bartlett
   (Old Bartlett Hotel)

10. Keyhole in the Conner Hotel
    (Connor Hotel)

11. Por Favor, Pull Up a Chair
    (Warehouse)

12. Don't Look Under the Bed
    (United Verde Hospital / Grand Hotel)

13. The Haunted Woods
    (Prescott National Forest)

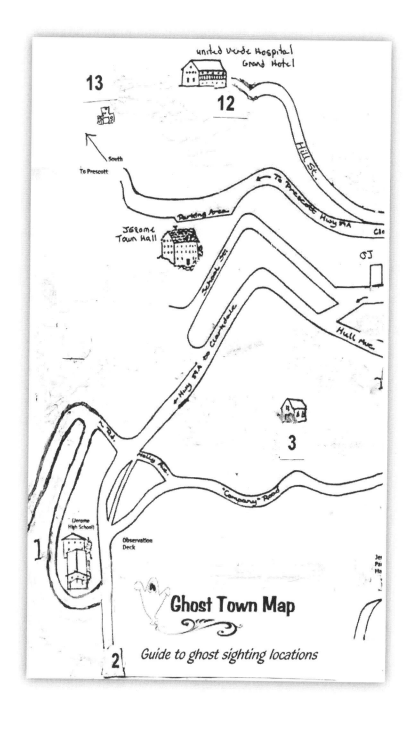

united Verde Hospital
Grand Hotel

13

12

Hill St.

South
To Prescott

← To Prescott Hwy 89A

Parking Area

Cle

Jerome
Town Hall

CJ

School St.

Hull Ave.

← Hwy 89A to Clarkdale

3

r. Rd.

Hull Ave.

"Company" Road

Jerome
High School

Observation
Deck

Jer
Par
Ha

1

Ghost Town Map

Guide to ghost sighting locations

2

Ghost Town Map

Guide to ghost sighting locations 11

1. Biker Hitchhiker
   (Across from the old gas station)

2. Roxana "The Gypsy Ghost"
   (Far esd of the old cemetery)

3. You Don't Need Your Bones
   (Mexican Quarters)

4. Maddy and the Muleskinner
   (Audrey Head frame at State Park)

5. Murdered Moonshiner
   (Sliding Jail)

6. The Wickedest Madam in the West.
   (The Cuban Queen Bordello)

7. Spirit of "Sammie Dean"
   (Husband's Alley)

8. An Opium Fiend Feline "China Doll"
   (English Kitchen)

9. New Year's Eve at the Bartlett
   (Old Bartlett Hotel)

10. Keyhole in the Conner Hotel
    (Conror Hotel)

11. Por Favor, Pull Up a Chair
    (Warehouse)

12. Don't Look Under the Bed
    (United Verde Hospital / Grand Hotel)

13. The Haunted Woods
    (Prescott National Forest)

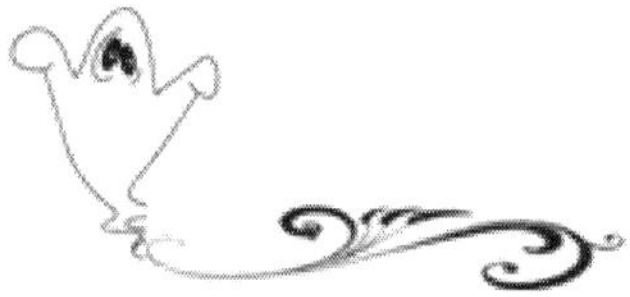

Biker Hitchhiker
Chapter 1

It was a rainy afternoon in March as I drove up the steep and winding road to Jerome. My fog lights were on and the windshield wipers could barely keep up with the pouring rain. As I rounded a sharp curve, my headlights flashed on a large man on the side of the road. He wore a black motorcycle jacket and leather chaps as he stood in the rain with his thumb out. It was an awful day for anyone to be stuck out on the road, so I pulled over to the shoulder, leaned across the front seat and opened the passenger door.

"Thanks Man", said the stranger as he struggled to fit into the front seat of my compact car.

I noticed that his face was bruised and his hands were scratched and covered with dried blood. I found the dried blood a little peculiar, considering how hard it was raining.

When he caught me looking at his injuries, he said, "Name's Larry Price, but my friends call me Luke. I totaled my Harley a couple miles up the road. I decided to pull into the old gas station and wait out the rain. Guess I hit a slick spot in the road and the bike went down. Anyway, I lost my helmet in the crash and I 'm going back to see if I can find it."

I drove a couple miles more when Luke pointed to an old abandoned gas station and said, "You can drop me off here,"

I pulled under the station's canopy out of the rain. As Luke got out of the car he said, "Thanks for the lift man." That's when I noticed something else a little strange. Luke was barefoot.

For the rest of the day I just couldn't stop thinking about the bizarre encounter with the biker hitchhiker. I wondered why the man, whom I had given a ride, wasn't wearing any boots.

Later that night, I stopped in at a local saloon called the Spirit Room and shared my story with the bartender.

"Did he mention his name?" Paul the bartender asked.

"As a matter of fact, he did. He said his name was Larry Price, but his friends called him Luke," I replied.

Paul looked at a calendar that hung on the wall. His face went pale.

"Are you sure he said Larry Price?"

I nodded, "That's what he said".

"Are you making this story up? 'Cause, if you are, I don't find it a bit funny. Luke was my friend. He died in a motorcycle wreck on March 8th, a year ago today. Luke lost control of his bike just before the old gas station. He was thrown over the handlebars. It was a terrible wreck. His helmet might have saved his life, but he hadn't buckled it. Coroner said that he was killed instantly. At least Luke didn't suffer."

Paul continued. "A bunch of us friends got together and placed a marker at the crash site. If you look to the hillside just before the old gas station, you'll see his name engraved on a stone marker and the pair of cowboy boots he was wearing that day he went down."

Paul handed me my beer. "Luke was a regular at this bar. He always sat on the very stool you're sitting on. Most of the guys that knew Luke leave that seat empty out of respect for him".

I knew that I told the truth, but the story of my strange encounter with the barefoot hitchhiker must have hit a raw nerve with the patrons. A couple big bikers sitting at the bar overheard my story and made a couple of intimidating comments.

I certainly wasn't there to start any trouble, so I gave Paul my condolences, moved to another seat and quickly finished my beer.

I'll never forget picking up that hitchhiker that rainy afternoon. And Paul was right; If you look on the hillside just before the old gas station, you'll see a weathered old pair of cowboy boots in front of a stone marker.

(Ghost boots photo by Josh Gray)

"Roxana"
The Gypsy Ghost
Chapter 2

Roxana's family traveled with a medicine show bringing various types of entertainment to western boomtowns. Their horse-drawn wagons were decorated with elaborate paint and filigree to add to the flair of the productions. Because of the transient nature of the job, many of the performers lived in these wagons full time.

ᵢer of 1912, they came to Jerome. The
ᵈed a so-called doctor selling his latest
bottle. Fortune tellers would gaze into
ᵢlls or consult tarot cards and for a price,
foreᵤ ᵼhe future. Women wearing gold bangles and colorful head scarves performed exotic dances. Roxana loved to dance and play the tambourine with the performers. To her, this was a way of life and in fact, the only life she knew.

The caravan of gypsies would stay until they wore out their welcome and then move on.

Roxana's mother died when she and her brother, Jimmy were very young. They were raised by their father, who was a con artist that sold "snake oil" to the sick and gullible. He was also a master pickpocket. They say he could steal your shoe laces right out of your shoes. He even trained their dog to steal chickens. Wherever they traveled, they could always count on a chicken for dinner.

Roxana's father taught his two children the art of pick pocketing so they could one day survive without him. He had his children practice several hours a day. One technique he used was to fasten pockets to quilts. In these pockets, he placed wallets, cash and jewels. Several small bells were sown to the pockets. Your touch had to be light enough to lift the items out without ringing the bells. It was all a matter of practicing the moves until they were smooth as silk.

Roxana's father had no respect for common thugs or robbers. He believed that pick-pockets were noble. He said, "Anybody can stick a gun in a person's face. That's not hard to do. But to take a person's money without them knowing it's gone, that's the art of it and the cleverness of it. It's a ballet of the fingers and the key is distraction and slight-of-hand."

It wasn't long before Roxana and her brother Jimmy became proficient at the craft of pick-pocketing. They often worked together. Roxana's job was to distract the unsuspecting target by asking a question, while her little brother would slip his hand into their pocket or purse and steal their valuables.

After Roxana's father died, Jimmy started hanging with the wrong crowd and became arrogant and greedy. He started robbing with a gun, which was of course, something his father warned him never to do. Pick-pocketing is petty theft and it's often dismissed by the courts with a warning. But if you're caught robbing with a weapon, you're going to jail.

Jimmy didn't listen to his father's advice and was ultimately killed by police in a bank heist.

Roxana stayed true to her craft, but with an added element. Her most effective distraction was sex appeal. She would dress attractively and hang around a saloon, usually pretending to be drunk. Most of her victims were drunken, lonely men, which made them easy targets. She would first engage by making small talk with the unsuspecting man. During the conversation, she would gently slide his wallet out, excuse herself and then slip away into the crowd.

Roxana past on many years ago and is now said to be a gypsy ghost. Gypsy ghosts are known to have the ability to travel through many dimensions and often keep their bad habits after death.

Roxana has been suspected of working the crowds in several tourist towns, including Jerome, lifting the valuables of unsuspecting visitors.

You might hear phantom footsteps as you walk down the sidewalk or feel a slight nudge. You turn, but no one's there. Don't be surprised if Roxana has just lifted your cash, credit card, camera, sun glasses, or wallet. With unseen hands, she may even slip your gold chain from your neck.

Shoppers distracted by their cell phones are especially easy prey. A bracelet, a watch, your favorite earrings or even your wedding ring may be gone in the blink of an eye.

There are skeptics who claim there is no such thing as a gypsy ghost, maintaining that the tourist must have had a lapse of memory. Or perhaps the tourist left their valuables behind at a bar or on a sales counter. They figure your missing money must have just fallen out of your pocket, the clasp broke on your expensive necklace or your ring simply slipped from your finger. Others, however, are very aware of Roxana the gypsy ghost and in fact, have even seen her in action.

Actually, being a ghost, Roxana has no need for your valuables. She may simply pick-pocket your things just to stay in practice. Or perhaps she just wants a little attention.

They say the only way to get your belongings back is to go to her grave in the old "Hogback Cemetery" and trade salt for your missing possessions.

Just follow the sound of the tambourine to the back of the graveyard. Beneath a mesquite tree you'll find her grave surrounded by an ornate wrought iron fence. Toss a handful of salt on her grave, reach through the iron rails and retrieve your missing things.

But a word of warning, if you pilfer something that is not yours from her grave, you will be unable to sleep until the new moon appears in the night sky. It is at that time when Roxana purges her grave of the unclaimed items.

Maddy and
The Muleskinner

Chapter 3

The United Verde Copper Company in Jerome, Arizona operated one of the most modern operations known at the time. In 1909, the Town of Jerome was supplied with electricity. By 1916, mules were no longer used in the tunnels and electric locomotives took their place hauling the precious ore to the newly constructed smelter in Clarkdale.

Mules played a large part in the long history of mining in the United States. These beasts of burden were sure-footed, sturdy animals with a first-rate amount of common sense. They stepped carefully over rails, rocks and timbers. These animals adapted well to their work in the mines and learned very quickly.

The general behavior of the mules depended mostly on the ability of the muleskinner. Getting a mule down a dark mineshaft was not an easy task.

For a couple days before making its journey to the bottom of the mine, the mule would be deprived of food and water. The animal was then totally wrapped in canvas, with only its nose exposed for breathing. If this was not done, there was danger of a ruptured bladder or even suffocation while being lowered into the depths of the mine. Because of the absolute darkness underground, the mules would eventually become blind. Getting a mule back up out of the mine was even more difficult then lowering them down.

Even though Jackson (Jack) Hicks was only twenty-five, he had earned his status among the other muleskinners. Mules tended to develop trusting relationships with their muleskinners. Seldom would a mule allow his trainer to put them into a dangerous situation. Jack's team of six mules had worked the morning shift for a little over four years, pulling heavy steel ore carts through the underground tunnels and working all morning with few breaks.

The mule he named Maddy was his favorite. She had a white spot on her right shoulder and a big white 'roman nose'. There was no other mule that looked like her.

It was almost noon on October 12, 1913. The morning shift was over and the men were on their way up out of the mine. Soon, the next group of miners would start their decent into this man made Hell they called "The Mine".

Jack was often the last person to come up out of the mine. He usually stayed behind to care for the mules. He scrubbed their hooves with a soapy mixture to keep the corrosive copper water from eating away at their feet.

Jack also made sure the mules were safely in their stalls and that they were well fed and had plenty of cool water to drink.

The townsfolk were going about their daily business above ground, when suddenly, the well known mule named Maddy came stampeding down the crowded Main Street. She was slipping and sliding, kicking and braying and franticly flapping her ears. The townsfolk stepped aside and gave this out of control beast a wide berth.

Someone in the crowd shouted, "Where's Jack the mule skinner?! He needs to get his mule under control before she hurts someone!"

Maddy turned and bolted off into the hills, seemingly disappearing into the distant clouds on the horizon. The miners were surprised to see Maddy above ground, because once a mule was put into a cage and lowered deep into the pitch-dark mine shafts, they usually stayed underground the rest of their lives. They became known as blind mules.

Unexpectedly, the mine's alarm rang out seven bells. There had been a cave-in down at the thousand foot level. They were not sure how many miners were trapped underground.

Each miner was assigned an identification tag with a number. This tag was taken off a board by the miner and placed around his neck as he entered the mine. When he exited the mine, the tag was then returned to the board. After a final check, all the men on the morning shift were accounted for, except one..... Jack the Muleskinner.

Immediately, men were lowered into the mine. They started digging and moving tons of earth. They dug well into the night, working feverishly to reopen the mine tunnel.

Finally, there came a shout. "We've broken through!"

Five of the mules were found alive in their stalls. Now, only Jack and Maddy were missing. For hours, they continued their search, digging and moving large boulders.

Finally, they found Maddy. Sadly though, she lay dead, crushed by a fallen timber. Then, good news flew like lighting through the crowd. "We found Jack! He's alive!

Jack was taken to the hospital with a broken leg and several bruised ribs. While recovering from his injuries, Jack recalled the events leading up to the cave-in.

"I think Maddy knew something was wrong that morning, so I let her set the pace. A reluctant mule can sometimes be warning you of danger, Jack explained. "I knew darn well not to push her too hard, or she'd stop dead in her tracks. Then there was no moving her until I bribed her with some sort of treat. Yea, I had Maddy pretty spoiled."

With tears in his eyes, Jack recalled one of Maddy's little routines. "Her enormous bulk took up the majority of the mine's five foot wide tunnel," he chuckled. "She would lean against the wall, blocking a miner from passing. If the miner thought he'd outsmart Maddy by going around the other side, Maddy would shift her weight and lean against the other side. It usually took a tasty treat, like an apple, a carrot or a chew of tobacco to pass by her and even then, a swift kick to the shins might be the only thanks she offered. Maddy could also hold grudges. Anyone who was mean or abusive to her would get a nasty kick or even a bite when she decided to take revenge."

Jack continued. "When I heard the rumbling, I started to run, but I tripped and fell. I looked up and saw Maddy break from her stall. She actually ran and stood over me, shielding me from the falling timbers. Then, a big beam gave way, and what seemed like tons of earth buried both of us.

Maddy and I were pinned to the ground. I thought for sure I'd meet my maker.

Wiping a tear from his eye, he finished by saying, "Maddy was my guardian Angel. She saved my life and I'll sure miss her".

It wasn't until after his recovery that Jack was told about the frightened mule that came stampeding down Main Street. The dozens of witnesses that morning had only one explanation. That run-a-way mule must have been Maddy's ghost warning everyone of the danger.

Every day since that tragedy occurred back in 1913, the town siren blows at 11:51am in memory of the many men and animals that lost their lives working in the underground mine.

And somewhere, a thousand feet underground, in an abandoned mine tunnel is a stone marker with the word Maddy engraved on it. People say, if you put your ear to the tunnel shaft wall, you can still hear Maddy breathe.

Audrey Headframe
at the
Jerome State Park
Jerome, Arizona
(If you want to look deep into a mine shaft, visit the Audrey Headframe at the Jerome State Park.)

The Audrey Headframe is located near the Jerome State Park and it is free to visitors. It is Arizona's oldest and largest remaining wooden headframe and was completed in 1918.

The structure was built atop the mine shaft and supported all the equipment like pulleys and cables that would raise or lower men, equipment, ore and supplies from the Little Daisy copper mine. The mine's superintendent named it "Audrey Headframe" after his adopted daughter, Audrey.

A glass platform, atop a lighted, concrete-lined shaft now allows visitors to look down between their feet into the depths of the vertical mine shaft some 1,900 feet below.

Between 1915 and 1938 almost 4 million tons of ore was extracted from the mine, producing 397,000 tons of copper, 221 tons of silver and 5½ tons of gold. Ore was brought to the surface, and then transported by train and mule train, to the railhead in Clarkdale, in the Verde Valley below.

Murdered Moonshiner

Chapter 4

Prohibition in Arizona went into effect on Jan. 1, 1915, five years before the national ban began. The 18th amendment made manufacturing, importing or the sale of liquor illegal in the U.S. from 1920 to 1933.

Prohibition was, by most accounts, a failure and quickly produced bootleggers, speakeasies, bathtub gin and rumrunners who smuggled daily supplies of alcohol to their customers. A quart of 180-proof moonshine would cost about $6.50.

Bootleggers were making moonshine in old mine tunnels, in kitchen sinks, basements, barns and even in outhouses. If caught, moonshiners usually had to pay a $500 fine or serve six months in jail.

It was also relatively easy to find a doctor in Jerome to sign a prescription for medicinal whiskey, which could be purchased at most drugstores.

Jerome's Police Chief John D. Crowe was constantly on alert for illegal bootlegging activity. Crowe approached Mr. Gamble, the postmaster and offered him a hefty reward if he would keep his eyes open for signs of bootleggers as he delivered the mail around town and the surrounding county.

One morning, while on his route delivering mail, Gamble took a shortcut through a back road and stumbled upon a gang of moonshiners making whiskey along Cherry Creek. He gave this information to officer Crowe for the reward.

As a result of Postmaster Gamble's information, Chief Crowe and his men captured three of the most elaborate stills ever seen. Two were on Oak Creek in Sedona, and the third was on Cherry Creek just south of Jerome. The Cherry Creek still was producing over four hundred fifty gallons in one batch and was claimed to be the largest operation ever encountered in the state of Arizona.

Jim Laughlin, a noted bootleg bandit, who was operating the still on Cherry Creek was captured and sentenced to six months in jail.

When Jim Laughlin found out that Chief Crowe had paid the Postmaster to rat him out, heated words were exchanged between the Chief and Jim. Jim pledged revenge when he got out of jail.

A few days later The Verde Copper Newspaper reported: "Postmaster Gamble, one of Jerome's most prominent citizens has been missing since last Friday.

His mail bag and lantern were found in front of the post office sometime Wednesday night. On top of the bag was a note pinched in the jaws of a mouse trap that said, INFORMANTS BEWARE. We kill rats and chuck their bodies down abandoned mine shafts."

It was presumed that Postmaster Gamble may have been murdered by one of the moonshiners and his body disposed of in exactly this manner.

Jim Laughlin was still in jail at the time of Gamble's disappearance. Chief Crowe believing that Laughlin may have information about what happened to Gamble, offered Laughlin a "get out of jail free card" if he would rat out his fellow moonshiner.

Laughlin alleged he knew nothing about the postmaster's disappearance and said he would rather rot in jail than become a snitch.

The next day Jim Laughlin was found stabbed to death in his locked cell. The murderer had written the words, "REVENGE IS MINE" in Laughlin's blood on the concrete wall of the cell. The assassin had to have had a jail key to enter. The incident was reported as a suicide, yet no weapon was found at the crime scene.

The jail at that time was located on Main Street and Hull Street. After Jim Laughlin's death in 1927, the jail was remodeled into two cells and the concrete walls were painted over. Mysteriously the blood stains kept reappearing after repeated coats of paint.

In the 1930's, an underground, man made explosion caused the Town's surface to shift and several buildings began to crumble, including the jail. The concrete jail began pulling away from the hillside.

The building was considered unsafe and the prisoners were relocated to other facilities. The concrete jail began to slowly move downhill by itself. It eventually slid 225 feet from its original location and finally came to rest in the middle of the street below. For years, the townsfolk simply drove around the jail.

The Town of Jerome eventually took on the task of the jail's preservation and moved it to its present location. It was stabilized with retaining walls and reinforcing bars.

Today, the jail is a tourist attraction, appropriately named the "Sliding Jail". The blood stained walls have all but faded, but Jim Laughlin's ghost remains.

The claim is, the jail reeks of moonshine, and Jim Laughlin's tormented spirit can still be heard crying out for justice from his cell. The infamous jail that once locked people inside, now, ironically barricades anyone from entering with a posted sign that reads "KEEP OUT".

You Don't Need Your Bones to Get to Heaven

Chapter 5

The landlord insisted on a year's lease, which was fine with me. There's not much choice in Jerome for a starving artist and I didn't plan on moving anytime soon anyway. He also warned me about the next door neighbors, claiming they were a little out of touch with reality.

Apparently, the neighbors maintained that the house was haunted; however the landlord assured me that this was just a fairy tale. I signed my lease and paid the deposit.

The house was built around 1910, but had been remodeled sometime in the thirties or forties. I noticed a strong smoky, musty type odor in the kitchen. It was the only part of the house that was still original. The kitchen had a heavy, old fashioned cast-iron sink and a few of the lower cabinet doors had been painted shut over the years and would not open. Being a single guy, I didn't have much stuff to stash in the cabinets anyway.

My favorite room was the dining room. It had a soft ambient light that would be perfect for my art studio. I was anxious to get a few paintings ready for the upcoming "Art Walk". I had the utilities turned on and moved in. That's when the nightmares started.

Each night I would have the same dream and each time it seemed more intense. I was losing sleep and after a few days I became absolutely exhausted. I had dark circles under my eyes, my chest was tight and my stomach felt rotten.

I knew that I needed to talk to someone about my persistent dream, so I called my friend Dave and asked him if would meet with me.

I explained the situation to him. "You know when you have a dream and wake up, your conscious mind takes over and the dream images quickly fade? Well that's not the case. The images stay with me and become more real every time I dream. It starts with a house on fire. Then I hear pots and pans rattling in the kitchen.

I look up and see two little girls standing at the foot of my bed. It's the very same dream, over and over and over. Then I think about it all day long. It's driving me crazy".

Dave, trying to be helpful, replied, "You know Mark, the neighbors might just be right. Maybe this house is haunted. My advice would be to move. You can't keep on like this. I can see it's really taking a toll on you."

I continued, "Last night the little blond girl mouthed the words "Help us". I closed my eyes and tried to ignore the dream and go back to sleep, but it was impossible. I got out of bed, made coffee and sat down at the dining room table just staring into the kitchen. The image in my dream was so real that I got out my art supplies and painted a portrait of the two little girls".

I removed a painting from the easel standing in the corner.

Looking at the portrait, Dave said, "The girls don't look like sisters. Maybe they were in this house when something tragic happened and now they're stuck in this dimension and need help to move on."

Dave offered to look through the town's archives and do a little investigation on the history of this house. He thought maybe he could find something that might be contributing to my nightmares. A few days later, Dave brought me a newspaper article he found in the archives.

Miner Journal; Prescott; Friday's Daily. June 12, 1918

The article was about the "Big Fire" that started the morning of June 6 in the Mexican Quarters.

Mines - Jou

Sunday, June 12, 1918

Hispanic Neighborhood Bur

For hours, a fire threatened to make a clean sweep through the Hispanic Neighborhood. Over 60 dwellings were destroyed when fire struck the Mexican Quarters in Jerome early Wednesday morning. The houses in that part of town are built closely together and of flimsy construction. The fire caused the death of two men, and two young girls are still unaccounted for.

Hispanic Neighborhood Burns

For hours, a fire threatened to make a clean sweep through the Hispanic Neighborhood. Over 60 dwellings were destroyed when fire struck the Mexican Quarters in Jerome early Wednesday morning. The houses in that part of town are built closely together and of flimsy construction. The fire caused the death of two men, and two young girls are still unaccounted for.

In this view, a crowd of concerned residents watch the fire of June 6, 1918 that burned 60 structures in the Hispanic neighborhood, leaving 1,000 people homeless and an untold amount in property damage.

Sunday, June 12, 1918

continued from page 1

In this view, a crowd of concerned residents watch the fire of June 6, 1918 that burned 60 structures in the Hispanic neighborhood, leaving 1,000 people homeless and an untold amount in property damage.

The newspaper article went on to say:

An elderly man named Jose Cervantes was a victim of the flames. Cervantes managed to get out of the fire, but his skin was burned from his body. He was taken to the U. V. hospital and passed away at 2:30 in the afternoon.

Trinidad Contreras, a single Mexican man, age 35, lay asleep on his cot at a rooming house. He had been drinking and apparently made no effort to get out of bed when the flames struck the house. It is believed that he suffocated before he could help himself.

A Fireman, passing the ruins of the house, noticed the charred trunk of Trinidad's body resting on a bed, but because of the heat, he could not get to the remains. All he could do was watch as the body was reduced to ashes.

The brave firefighters did everything they could to put out the fire. As soon as the ruins of the fire cool off, they will perform an intense search for the missing girls. Please pray for the girls and their families.

Fire Chief Homer made a public announcement in Jerome's Upper Park around 10:00 AM on Monday.

"Because of the extent of this tragedy, I know this fire has had an enormous impact on our community. Two men are confirmed dead and losing two girls in one tragic event is hard for us all to accept".

Chief Homer went on to say "On Sunday, every inch of the rubble was thoroughly searched and yet, there was no trace of the missing girls. Homer said, "Sometimes when young children feel heat and smell smoke, they get scared and are likely to hide. We find them under beds, closets, in crawl spaces and in bathtubs. We've looked in every conceivable place for these two girls and I'm confident they were not burned up in the fire. Where they are now, however, is a mystery.

Everyone seems to have an opinion about the fire, but these are the facts. The fire started in an upstairs bedroom of a wood framed house. The house was occupied by a Mexican family named Salvador. Angelina Salvador was celebrating her 9th birthday with her friend Alice Olsen, age 10.

The Olsen girl was sleeping over. It appears that the girls were playing with a burning candle and in the pre-dawn hours of the morning, caught their bed on fire.

Mrs. Salvador woke up early to the smell of smoke coming from her daughter's room. She immediately woke her husband and grabbed their sleeping baby. Mr. Salvador ran into their daughter's bedroom and saw the bed in flames. Thankfully, the girls were not in it. A quick search under the bed and in the closet confirmed the girls were not in the bedroom. They ran through the house screaming and franticly searching for the two girls. After throwing several buckets of water on the kitchen, they ran into the street, barely escaping the flames. They watched in horror, not knowing where the girls were, as the raging inferno consumed their home. Only a small portion of the Salvador's kitchen was spared in the blaze.

The out of control fire then quickly spread to the nearby homes and in a blink of an eye, the entire Mexican Quarter was on fire."

The chief concluded, "I want to thank the Fire fighters and all the volunteers who have opened their homes to the victims of this fire. We will continue to search for the missing children."

After reading Dave's article, it definitely shed some light on the mysterious nightmares I'd been having.

Even though the "big fire" happened over a hundred years ago, I just knew that those kitchen cabinets had some odd connection to those little girls.

It's my belief that once the fire started, the girls were scared and crawled into the corner cabinet to hide. Before they knew it, they were both overcome by the smoke.

Sadly, they both died in that cabinet of smoke inhalation. The girl's souls are still waiting in limbo. They need to be released from the anguish and guilt they hold for starting the fire that burned the Mexican Quarter down.

 I'm not a preacher or an exorcist, but I wanted to try to help the girls move on. I did the only thing I knew to do. I repainted the portrait of the two girls, only this time, I painted them ascending into heaven.

I laid the portrait on the kitchen counter and told the girls that all had been forgiven and they did not need their bones to get to heaven.

I asked if they would give me a sign when they completed their journey.

The next day I awoke with the afternoon sun blazing in my face. For the first time in months I had slept through the night and even late into the morning. As I stumbled into the kitchen for my coffee, I noticed that the portrait was missing from the counter and the corner cabinet door, the one that was painted shut, was wide open.

I pushed the cabinet door closed with my foot and secured the door with a big screw.

I shivered to think that their bones were still there, and I couldn't bring myself to even look.

I'm actually at peace knowing that the girl's remains may still be in my cabinet. All I know is that the dreams have stopped and my paintings are now selling. I'm sure I helped those two little girl's spirits to move on..., because I know, you don't need your bones to get to heaven.

The Wickedest Madam
In the West

Chapter 6

The wickedest Madam to set foot in the dusty mining town of Jerome was a woman named Anita Gonzales, AKA the Cuban Queen. She began her trade in the red light district of Storyville, in New Orleans in the early 1900s. It was there, where she met and married the famous Jelly Roll Morton, (*the self-proclaimed inventor of jazz*).

They traveled the country, setting trends in both fashion and music during the infancy of the jazz age.

In 1922, after an explosive break-up, Jelly Roll Morton went to Chicago and she headed for the untamed West. She settled in Arizona, in a rich, copper mining camp called Jerome. Of the fifteen thousand people residing in the town, ninety percent of them were men. That was excellent odds for her type of business.

She had come to Jerome for the same reason everyone else did... to seek her fortune.

Her mining technique was, however, a little different. Instead of mining the earth, she would be mining the pockets of the miners.

She opened up a house of prostitution in the red-light district, and called it, "The Cuban Queen Bordello". She ruled supreme for a decade in this rough and tumble Arizona mining town during the Roaring Twenties.

During Jerome's more corrupt times, brothels and bordellos could be found just about everywhere. Later, however, when the town decided to exist in a more "civilized" manner, these houses of ill repute were banned from Main Street.

Most were relocated two blocks off Main, to what was designated as "The Red Light District". This area was filled with women whose business was to provide "entertainment" to the many miners of this rowdy city. At one point, it was estimated that more than 100 prostitutes practiced their trade in Jerome.

Old timers remember the Cuban Queen as a beautiful dark skinned, curvaceous, well-dressed madam.

She was possibly *mulatto*, who spoke with a pronounced Southern accent in an alluring soft voice. Some said she was a little mysterious and was deeply rooted in her Haitian ancestry traditions of practicing *Voodoo and* Black Magic. She always carried a deck of Tarot cards in her pocket book and a pistol in her garter.

She was an expert at making money. She sold moonshine to the men, making sure they were liquored up so they were loose with both their morals and their cash.

She also charged her working girls for the use of their rooms, meals, laundry, doctor visits and any clothes provided them. She demanded to know every "john" that came and went, because she was entitled to a forty percent commission on each of the girls' services.

It is believed that in 1927 the Cuban Queen caught one of her Mexican working girls, Guadalupe with a john that wasn't paying for his service.

An incident took place in a little "crib" room in the Cuban Queen Bordello. The Cuban Queen pulled her pistol and fired a warning shot, accidently killing Guadalupe and wounding the john who was in bed with her.

The Cuban Queen and her accomplice abruptly slipped out of town and were never heard from again. Her evil deeds, however, did not end there. On the way out of town she kidnapped Guadalupe's three year old son, Enrique and claimed him as her own.

Guadalupe's family immediately went to the authorities, suspecting the madam may have taken him. No investigation was done and the family feared the madam may have bribed the authorities as she had often done before.

Being so young at the time of the kidnapping, Enrique forgot that he had a sister and three brothers back in Jerome, Arizona. Enrique was taken to Canyonville, Oregon and he lived out the rest of his life never knowing that his real mother had been murdered by the woman he was now calling mother.

In 1953, the copper mines of Jerome closed and Guadalupe's family moved away. They never lost hope though, of finding Enrique. They wrote numerous letters to the authorities, trying to get information on the madam and their missing relative. Unfortunately, the kidnapping remained unsolved for the next 80 years. It wasn't until 2003 when a real-estate agent, doing a title search on the Cuban Queen Building, found one of the letters from the family. This find, led her to an investigation of the madam and eventually solved the cold case from 1927. This information has been documented in a book titled, "<u>The Ghost of The Cuban Queen Bordello</u>" by Peggy Hicks..

After ninety years, The Cuban Queen's Bordello still stands on the edge of what was once, The Red Light District of Jerome.

The neighborhood watched as the Cuban Queen Bordello crumbled before their eyes, the rotting porch, the caved-in roof and the broken windows.

The only window that seemed to survive the test of time was a window on the upper balcony on the back side. This window was made of an unusual early bullet proof glass infused with chicken wire.

The neighbors agreed that from time to time, a shadowy figure of a dark skinned woman seemed to appear in the window. Not much thought was given to the matter though, because strange things like this frequently happen in Jerome.

Over time the window casement itself began to decay and one stormy night the bullet proof window came crashing to the ground. Remarkably, the glass panes did not break. The window lay in a pile of rubble for more than a decade as the building itself continued to crumble.

The recent owner, concerned with the integrity of the historic building installed a wrought iron fence around the structure to keep trespassers out and prevent further vandalism. The unusual bullet proof window was salvaged from the rubble with all nine window panes intact.

That window is now on display at the Arizona Discoveries Rock Shop at 317 Main Street, Jerome, Arizona.

Soon after the window was moved to its current location, strange things began to happen. The iron fence may have kept out the living intruders, but it did not hamper the paranormal.

It is believed that unsettled sprits will often attach themselves to inanimate objects, such as a toy, antique jewelry, furniture, a painting or even a window.

Apparently the undead spirit of Guadalupe, still tormented by the uncertainty of what happened to her child, continues to watch from the window.

The bullet proof Bordello window located in the Arizona Discoveries Rock Shop is now one of the "hot spots" on the ghost tours.

Visitors and ghost hunters alike are welcome to see the old window during business hours. However, keep in mind; photos of the window are not permitted. Spirits dislike the flash of a camera or the click of a shutter.

Many of Jerome gift shops, art galleries, restaurants, bars, hotels and wine tasting rooms are alleged to also have episodes of paranormal activity.

Friendly ghost tour guides, chosen for their storytelling abilities and historical knowledge of the town, give daily and nightly tours. Guests, armed with sensors, *EMF* detectors and digital cameras, search known locations for ghostly activity.

When the doors and windows are boarded up, how can you look through to the past? When all the old timers die, who will share their stories? And when all the old buildings are reduced to rubble, where will the ghost's reside?

Spirit of "Sammie Dean"

Chapter 7

Sammie Dean was a beautiful woman. Divorced, and in her late twenties, she was living the high life as a high class prostitute during Jerome, Arizona's rich copper mining days.

She owned a car, wore flashy jewelry, expensive furs and posh hats. Sammie Dean always had high profile and influential gentlemen callers.

She was well liked and a good friend to all the girls that worked in the red light district. Sammie knew of several women that had fallen prey to drunken men who had robbed and beat them. Some had even lost their lives to the men they entertained. She feared for her own safety, but in a town this corrupt, who was she to turn to? Sammie could only express her concerns in the letters to her trusted sister.

On a sultry summer night in 1931, Sammie Dean was found murdered in one of Jerome's classier bordellos.

An investigation revealed numerous fingerprints around the room. Bruises were found on her right arm and there were teeth marks on her breasts. There was plenty of evidence that Sammie had struggled for her life, but she had not been robbed. Her beaded hand purse was still on the night stand and her valuables remained untouched. There were no signs of forced entry, and it was apparent that Sammie had entertained her assassin that evening.

It was also clear that Sammie had been strangled to death. Her own silk stocking was found tied tightly around her neck.

But, even more disturbing, was that her murderer took the time to tie the silk stocking into an elaborate bow as if she was a gift for someone.

One of the clues left behind was a partially smoked Cuban cigar left in an ashtray. The investigators began to pull together a long list of men that smoked that particular brand of cigars.

Immediately, Sammie Dean's next of kin was notified. Upon hearing the terrible news, her sister came to Jerome to claim Sammie's body and take her back to Texas for burial.

Sammie's sister gave investigators the stack of letters Sammie had written. She thought there might be information contained in the letters that could help identify the murderer and bring him to justice.

One of the letters contained a list of men's names that Sammie had entertained in the past. One of the men was a waiter that worked for the New York Café. There was also a mining engineer, a prize fighter, a deputy sheriff and several other Jerome elites on the list.

The most disturbing letter had to do with the mayor and his son. Sammie claimed that the mayor's son was deeply in love with her and had even asked for her hand in marriage. But when he found out that his father, the mayor, was also a client of Sammie's, the son went into a jealous rage.

It was shortly after the investigators reviewed all the letters, when mysteriously, and for no apparent reason, the murder investigation was halted.

The numerous men on the list, who were allegedly using Sammy Dean's service, did not appear to have been contacted at all.

The case simply went cold. The mayor's son abruptly left town and was never questioned. The Mayor, who had been campaigning for re-election, pulled out of the race.

Today, the murder of Sammie Dean remains unsolved and her assassin unpunished. Someone got away with murder and carried their secret all the way to the grave.

The question still remains. Who strangled Sammie Dean? Was her death a crime of passion? And did a politician pay hush money to keep the investigation quiet?

The historic red light district where Sammie Dean was murdered is also known as "Husband's Alley". One can find it just below Main Street, as you enter Diaz Street.

This area is now overgrown with trees called "Las Aventuras "or sometimes called, "Trees of Hell". Strange shadows resembling silk stockings tied into bows have been seen hanging from the branches.

These bows seem to morph into clusters of leaves with the morning light.

Visitors wandering through this area after dark have reported paranormal phenomenon, including smoke curling in the air and the lingering smell of a cigar. Local ghost hunters have concluded that "Husband's Alley" is haunted by the ghosts of both Sammie Dean and her ruthless murderer.

It is probably wise to avoid snooping around husband's alley after dark. In fact, for your own safety, it's probably wise not to poke too far into this unsolved case either. It is said that the spirit of Sammie Dean's assassin is a merciless and vengeful one.

If you decide, however, that you must go digging into this unsolved case, be prepared for the consequences.

A few daring souls have ventured into the unknown and were sorry they did. Not long into their investigation, they began to experience the sensation of choking and felt something tightening around their own necks.

They soon found it very hard to breathe and abandoned their search.

It is believed that, even though Sammie Dean's body is buried back in Texas, the spirit of this former, well known prostitute still walks the streets of Jerome. Following close behind her and puffing on his cigar is Sammie's assassin, making sure that this case remains unsolved.

Most likely, we will never know exactly what happened on that fatal summer night and perhaps it's better left that way.

An Opium Addicted Feline
"China Doll"

Chapter 8

Today, Jerome, Arizona's one hundred year old English Kitchen Restaurant is doing business as Bobby D's BBQ. It is a full-service restaurant offering tasty, slow-smoked barbecue using an authentic old Hickory rotisserie smoker.

Oddly enough, The English Kitchen was originally a Chinese restaurant. It was built of adobe, on leased land in 1899 by Charley Hong.

The management of the restaurant remained in Chinese hands for decades. Mr. Yee Hong Song managed the English Kitchen for fifty years, from 1920 until his death in 1973. He was its sole waiter, chef, and dishwasher. He was always easy to spot, wearing the same clothes; a skirt-like white pants, black slippers, a calf length stained white apron and a chef's hat.

Often you could find Mr. Yee in a back booth under a cloud of blue opium smoke.

Eating at the English Kitchen was always somewhat of an adventure. The menu was usually different from day to day. Sometimes, a customer might not even know what he was getting until the food actually arrived at the table.

Although Mr. Yee lived in Jerome for over fifty years, he apparently never learned to speak English. In fact, he was almost unintelligible. It was thought by many, however, that Mr. Yee actually knew much more than he let on.

When Mr. Yee Hong Song died, the town folks tolled Jerome's bell and drove his hearse down Main Street. It was an unusual gesture of love and respect for him.

Although there is no clear "Chinatown" in Jerome, the 1900 census showed that of the 2,800 people living in Jerome, there were 60 Chinese citizens. By the 1920's, Jerome's population exploded to more than 15,000 and at that time, there were at least 14 Chinese restaurants in town.

The Chinese typically followed the growing railroad construction in the U.S., and also attached themselves to mining communities where they could find work and other opportunities.

The Chinese in Jerome were mostly viewed with mixed reactions and the predominately western townsfolk were not always so hospitable toward them. They were frequently described as "Celestials", along with other less flattering names.

Most of the Chinese were, of course, law abiding citizens who worked hard to establish a place for themselves out on the American frontier.

Chinese laborers known as "Coolies" had come to America bringing not only their dreams, but also their vices to our shores. One of these vices was opium. Even though opium was already used for medicinal purposes in America, the Chinese were the ones who brought it with them and introduced it for recreational use.

The coolies purchased opium from a network of Chinese dealers known as the "Tongs". The Tongs became the middlemen between the Chinese immigrants and their homeland where the opium was grown.

In 1900, the cost of an addict's daily supply was 50 cents, when the average wage was less than one dollar a day. Opium dens proved to be a very lucrative business for the Chinese.

The Chinese began digging underground tunnels from business to business, cellar to cellar and literally living and working in the tunnels they had dug. Their dens were set up in backrooms, laundries and basements of various Chinese-owned establishments.

The Jerome Times reported, "The opium dens of Jerome have literally gone underground."

Most often, much like those of Hong Kong and old Peking, the men and women associated with the dens were considered the scum of society, together with prostitutes, murderers, tramps and thieves.

After Mr. Yee's death, the English kitchen was sold. The new owners, Tom and his wife, ran the successful restaurant for the next twenty years. Soon after acquiring the business, strange things began to happen. A skinny, pesky, hollow eyed, white cat with a black spot on her left side kept hanging around the restaurant property.

Tom, assuming that the cat belonged to Mr. Yee and had been left behind after his death, named the cat "China Doll." Tom felt sorry for the cat and tried to feed her, but the cat would not eat. It seemed the cat wanted something else. Whenever he tried to pet her, she would leap just out of reach.

Then, one night the lights started to flicker off and on and unexplainable noises were heard below the restaurant. Tom's troubles continued until one evening when the English Kitchen went dark.

Tom thought his modern appliances might be overloading the electric system, so with flash light in hand, he went looking for the source of the trouble. He followed the wires to an unused storage room beneath the restaurant.

There were piles of rubbish, rusted pieces of sheet metal and dozens of rotted boards leaning up against the back wall. As Tom continued to follow the wires, he noticed a hidden, four foot high door standing partially open behind the debris. All of a sudden, the cat, "China Doll" came bounding through the opening.

Tom, a little shaken, took a deep breath and squeezed his way through the doorway. He found himself standing in a musty, old, underground opium den.

The only thing in the room was a few bunk beds and an old trunk. Beyond this room was a crumbling tunnel opening and Tom dared not go any further.

The dust covered bunks against the wall were now empty

A camelback trunk sat at the foot of one of the bunks. Tom opened the trunk. He could see that it was full of all kinds of paraphernalia. There was a dozen or so slender glass tubes, wrapped in Chinese paper that once contained opium. There were burners, clay bowls and a number of pipes used for smoking the opium.

In the trunk, there were also several faded photos dating back to the early 1900's. One photo was of two Chinese men, resting on a bed, apparently not feeling any pain.

The story of the opium trade is an ugly one. Inside this dark and dreary, airless den was where men and women curled up both day and night on these soiled beds. It was here, they would adoringly toast these tiny lumps of delight, transporting themselves, temporarily at least, into their own drug induced paradise. It also, however, soon would transport the user into the assured hell of addiction.

Another photo particularly caught Tom's interest. It was of a Chinese man holding a white cat with a black spot on her left side.

The cat in the photo was clearly the same cat Tom had named China Doll.

"China Doll," addicted to the vapors of the opium drug is now traveling the underground tunnels of Jerome, hiding under porches and in back alleys looking for that illusive puff of blue smoke.

Is it possible that "China Doll" will live forever as opium addicted ghost kitty?

New Year's Eve at the Bartlett

Chapter 9

Today the Bartlett Hotel is a local landmark, owned by the Jerome Historical Society. Now secured by steel bars, all that remains is the shell of a once beautifully constructed building,

For entertainment, visiting tourists toss coins through the bars at an old outhouse and some rusted mining artifacts.

During an annual event called "The Ghost Walk", the ruins are used as a stage for lively performances held by the Jerome Historical Society.

The original building was built in 1901. It was an elaborate Hotel with twenty rooms. Each room was decorated lavishly, each in a different color scheme. A bank, a drug store, and a newspaper office called "The News," operated on the sub-level along First Street.

The building became unstable after the landslides in the 1930's and was abandoned in the 1940's. In the 1950's, the mining company sold portions of the hotel for salvage.

A demolition crew was hired to remove the unstable top floors of the building. In the process, a large, heavy unclaimed wardrobe trunk was found in a closet. Across the top of the lid was a piece of tape with the words "Miss Abigail Gordon's costume and makeup case".

It was exciting to imagine what treasures and antiques waited inside. The keys to the lock were long gone and a decision was made to break into the trunk.

The inside was lined with an expensive blue velvet lining that was in amazing shape for its age.

In the top drawer, there was a 14 karat gold plated cigarette case, an ivory cigarette holder and two ticket stubs to an orchestra performance at the Sam H. Harris Theatre in Chicago. It was dated, SAT. EVE. OCT. 11, 1930.

In the second drawer, there was a large, single ostrich feather and a pair of ladies, black, leather lace-up boots from the late 1920's.

Oddly, the boot string of the left boot was missing. The bottom drawer of the trunk was stuck shut and had to be forced open.

In the bottom drawer was a bundle, wrapped in a decaying newspaper dated Jan 1, 1931. After removing the crumbling newspaper, the bundle appeared to be wrapped again in a woman's whale-bone corset.

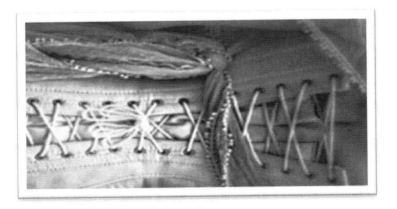

Inside the corset was something no one was expecting. It was the remains of a mummified infant.

Some of its red hair was still attached to the skull. The infant was dressed in a gown made from a pillowcase and a diaper made from a wash cloth. The initials B H, presumably for the Bartlett Hotel were embroidered on both.

The local police and the Yavapai County Coroner were called to investigate. They checked records for the name Abigail Gordon' from that time period, but came up with nothing.

The coroner determined that the remains were that of a newborn girl and had been in the trunk for approximately 20 years. She had been delivered at full term, but apparently not in a hospital, because the baby's umbilical cord was still attached. The umbilical cord had been tied off with a black shoestring matching the string on the right boot found in the trunk. The Coroner believed that the child lived about a week and may have had some physical issues. The cause of death could not be determined. The trunk, however, did offer many clues as to who this Miss Abigail Gordon may have been.

It seemed that Miss Abigail must have been some sort of entertainer and perhaps came to Jerome to perform in a vaudeville act at one of the town's theaters.

The pair of ladies black, leather lace-up boots had metal taps on the bottom used for tap dancing. Also, she may have been wealthy, taking into consideration the gold cigarette case, the ivory cigarette holder and expensive tickets to the orchestra performance in Chicago.

The most disturbing question is; why was this small corpse wrapped in a woman's corset and left behind in a wardrobe trunk? Was the corset also a clue as to what had happened to the infant?

Did Miss Abigail Gordon wear a tight corset to minimize the size of her waist and conceal her pregnancy while she performed?

In the 1920's, there was explicit medical advice that the tight lacing of a corset could harm a developing fetus. Doctors were also aware of the ill effects that smoking had on a growing fetus. An early study noted that when a pregnant mother smoked, the fetal heartbeat raised abruptly, an effect then called "tobacco heart".

Could Miss Abigail Gordon have ignored the advice of doctors just to advance her career, and all at the expense of her unborn child?

Some have concluded that Abigail may have tried to conceal her daughter's very existence. The question was, once her daughter was born, could she have callously placed the infant in a drawer to muffle her cries while she performed on stage? If so, did she return one night, only to find that her child was dead? These are questions that will probably never be answered.

Nevertheless, it is believed that Miss Abigail's undead spirit, haunted by her evil deeds, returns to Jerome every New Year's Eve to celebrate the coming of a new year. Undetected, she intermingles with the party goers, laughing, drinking champagne and ringing in the New Year.

But when the music stops, the lights are turned off and the crowd goes home, Miss Abigail returns to the Bartlett filled with sorrow and remorse. She spends the rest of the night sifting through the debris looking and listening for her baby girl's faint cries.

People have long reported seeing a woman with an hour-glass figure, walking through the corridors of the Bartlett Hotel in the pre-dawn hours of New Years Eve. Then, before the break of dawn on January 1st, Miss Abigail Gordon vanishes.

If you missed Miss Abigail Gordon this year, don't worry. It's almost certain that she will return to the Bartlett Hotel next New Years Eve as she has done for the last seventy five years.

Happy New Year!

Keyhole in the Connor Hotel

Chapter 10

George was traveling by car, across the country. As evening fell, he became tired and stopped in a small mountain town in central Arizona. He rented a room for the night at a place called The Connor Hotel before continuing on his journey.

With his small suitcase in one hand and the room key in the other, he walked up the stairs and made his way down the hall.

Shiny brass numbers were nailed above each of the room doors. The odd numbers 1, 3, 5 and 7 were on the right side of the hall, and even numbers 2, 4, and 8 were on the left. George could see the imprint of the number 6 on the appropriate door, but the brass number was missing.

As he walked by the unmarked room, he had a weird feeling and noticed what seemed to be a rancid odor in the air. George felt a wash of cold air blow across the floor at the cuff of his pants.

Shaking off the creepy feeling, he checked the number on his room key. It was number eight. He continued to his room and unlocked the door.

The old hotel was a little outdated, however, his room looked quite clean and comfortable. George was tired, so he wasted no time. He brushed his teeth, slipped on his night clothes, climbed into bed, and fell asleep.

In the middle of the night, George awoke shivering. He sniffed the air. That rancid smell he noticed earlier was now drifting under the door into his room. He got up, cracked the window and turned up the heat, but nothing seemed to help.

George called the front desk to complain, but got no response. Determined to get some answers, he climbed out of bed and made his way down the hall. As he walked past the unmarked room, the rancid smell intensified.

Filled with curiosity, he took a closer look. The light from the hallway revealed that the door had been screwed shut from the outside long ago. George bent over and put his eye to the keyhole. Nothing seemed out of the ordinary about the room, but he immediately moved from the door when he noticed the silhouette of a woman curled up on the bed, asleep.

George continued to the hotel lobby to make his complaint. The night clerk's only solution was more blankets. George, now a little upset, vowed to take the issue up with management in the morning. With arms laden with blankets, he climbed back up the stairs.

On his way to his room, he stopped again at the unmarked door. He put his eye to the keyhole again, but this time, quickly drew back. The keyhole was filled with something red.

He figured that the woman, sensing a peeping Tom, must have covered the key hole with red tape or paper. George hurried to his room. Once in his room, he rolled up a bath towel and wedged it against the bottom of the door hoping it would keep the awful smell out. The rest of the night, he tossed and turned and even had nightmares about the woman in the unmarked room.

The next morning, with his suitcase packed, he descended the staircase to the hotel lobby. George looked straight at the young man at the front desk, "Excuse me. I'd like to speak with the manager."

"One moment please. I'll see if she's in," replied the young man.

A few moments later, a sickly looking woman with ashy white skin, dark glasses and a scarf around her neck came to the counter. In a ragged voice, the woman said, "I'm the manager. What can I do for you sir?"

George adamantly complained about his cold sleepless night. He also wanted answers about the unmarked room and the rancid smell.

"That room has been vacant for more than a hundred years", replied the manager.

George responded, "Well, you might think it's vacant, but I looked in the keyhole and there was a woman sleeping in there. The next time I tried to look, the woman had covered the keyhole with red tape or a piece paper."

The manager cleared her throat, raised an eyebrow at George and said, "So, you make it a habit of peeking into other people's rooms? Sir, your mind must have been playing tricks on you… or maybe it was a ghost".

George snapped back, "I saw what I saw and I don't believe in ghosts. I want an answer and I want my money back too. I had a horrible night in this creepy place."

"If you must know I'll tell you. But you'll probably wish you had never asked," said the manager.

"Back in 1898 when the Connor Hotel first opened, a beautiful young woman was murdered in Room Six. Her assassin broke into her room, raped her, slit her throat and then stabbed her in the eye with his pocket knife. He stole her valuables, then jumped out the second story window and disappeared.

"The young woman lay dead in her blood soaked bed for several days before she was discovered. The room was boarded up and it's been vacant ever since. No one has dared open it."

"That young woman's spirit is still trapped in that room. She's bloodless and white as a sheet, except for her red eye. Her bloody eye is always watching for the man that did this to her."

As the woman manager leaned forward, George could smell her rancid breath. It was the very same stench that had drifted from the unmarked room last night. The manager then lifted the corner of her dark glasses, just enough for George to see a bloody red eye.

George now realized that it was not a red piece of tape on the Keyhole, but the bloody eye of the manager that was staring back at him last night.

He was so spooked; he ran out the door and swore he would never complain about a room again.

In the 2000 The Conner Hotel was renovated. The hotel now provides all the modern amenities while keeping its historic splendor.

Por Favor, Pull Up a Chair

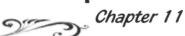

Chapter 11

Leroy was sick to death of his corporate job. He had fought his way up the ladder from sales to management, stepping on toes and brown-nosing.

Yes, he had it all, the fancy house, the fast car and a young secretary that did anything he asked.

Leroy knew that he drank too much, smoked too much and took too many pills. It's a wonder his wife stayed married to him for as long as she had. It had only been a few months after a nasty divorce that his ex-wife married another man. His own two kids were now calling that man, Dad.

Leroy was now just a shell of a man in a business suit. He now questioned the reason for his very existence. He was ready to put a gun to his head and end it all. Stopping by the liquor store in his Ferrari one evening, he bought a bottle of Southern Comfort and drove off into the night.

Having no sense of time or direction, he pulled off the interstate onto historic 89A. He drove until the road ended in an old mining town. Leroy pulled over, got out of the car and looked around.

The full moon illuminated the cold night and seemed to cast eerie shadows on everything. He could see a few lights in the distance, yet he had no idea where he was. The night was deathly quiet. He thought to himself, "Even the cricket population must be dead this time of year."

Off to the side was an old abandon building, perhaps a warehouse of some kind. He noticed several pieces of old mining equipment left to rust in the ground. Leroy lit a cigarette, retrieved his pistol from beneath the seat and stuffed it into his pants pocket. He grabbed the brown paper bag with the half consumed bottle of Southern Comfort and wandered over to the building to investigate.

The windows were all broken out and the door stood open. The similarities to his life were intriguing. An empty shell of a once important building paralleled the way he felt about himself. "This might be just the place to end it all," he mumbled to himself.

Leroy looked inside and noticed a set of mismatched chairs around an old wooden table parked in the shadows. He walked over to the table, pulled out a chair and sat down. He found it odd that the table appeared clean considering everything else in the room was covered with a thick layer of dust.

He took a swig of Southern Comfort and read the label. Somehow the bottle was true to its name. The liquor felt like an old friend and gave him some warmth and comfort from the cold lonely night.

When he sat the bottle down, he was more than startled when he noticed a scruffy Mexican man sitting at the other end of the table. He had not heard the stranger walk in and he was positive the man was not there when he took a seat at the table.

Leroy announced to the Stranger, "If you came to stop me from ending it all, you can just forget it. My mind's made up."

The Mexican man replied, "Oh, I think it's a good idea. You'll get no argument from me, amigo. I'm just here for our poker game."

Leroy found the stranger staring at the bottle of Southern Comfort.

"Care for a drink?" Leroy offered him the bottle.

"No gracias, replied the Mexican. "I haven't had a drink in 70 years. But believe me; I used to stay drunk all the time. In fact, I actually drank myself to death."

Leroy was puzzled at what the Mexican man said.

Seemingly appearing from nowhere, two more men silently took a seat at the table; a short Chinaman and a man in a doctor's coat with a stethoscope hanging around his neck.

"What's going on here?" Leroy demanded. "If this is one of those interventions, it's not going to work. Nothing you can say or do will stop me from killing myself."

The Mexican remarked, "As I said before, we're all just here for our Saturday night poker game. Let me introduce you to my friends. This here is the Chinaman. He used to own a laundry and peddle opium. He's sort of a victim of his own doing, an overdose. Doc here was the chief surgeon at the hospital. He was just tired of life and gave himself a lethal dose of his own medicine."

He continued, "And the tall man standing behind you, waiting for you to get out of his chair so we can start the game is called High Pockets. He found his wife with another man and bludgeoned both of them to death with a pick axe. He was found guilty and sentenced to life in prison. He escaped his life's punishment by hanging himself in his jail cell. And of course, as I said before, I drank myself to death. You see, in one way or another, we all committed suicide and now we're all ghosts."

Frightened, Leroy jumped out of High Pocket's chair and threw his bottle of Southern Comfort against the wall.

The bottle shattered and the unconsumed liquor disappeared into the dusty floor. His action drew no response from the four men as they calmly continued to play cards.

Leroy felt a chill run deep through his bones. He knew something about this situation was very strange. He ran to his car, jumped in and turned the key. Click, click, click. The car battery was dead.

Now, even more frustrated, Leroy blurted, "Now I'm stuck in the middle of nowhere with a dead battery and my own head's playing tricks on me. Ghosts? How pathetic. There's no such thing as ghosts."

Leroy, more determined than ever to end it all, took the pistol from his pocket, put it in his mouth and squeezed the trigger. The blast of the gun was louder than anything he had ever heard. Then everything seemed to go into slow motion. He felt the excruciating pain of his ear drums bursting as the shot pierced the silent night and echoed through the hills. He felt his skull split wide open as the blood spewed from his body. His heart sounded like a bass drum beating and beating. It pumped and pumped until there was no more blood and then it stopped.

The moonlit night turned black and in an instant, as if transported in time, Leroy found himself standing next to the car, looking at the scene.

The Ferrari's windows were splattered in blood and there was a man slumped over the steering wheel with a gaping hole through his head. But seeing this mayhem brought on no emotion to Leroy, good or bad. All he knew is that he wasn't cold anymore. He wasn't sad or angry or depressed.

He wasn't thirsty or hungry. He felt nothing. Leroy was just an empty shell of a man in an overstuffed business suit.

Unexpectedly, Leroy found himself back in the warehouse at the poker table again. The Mexican looked up and saw Leroy standing there and said.

"Hey, amigo; nice to see you again. We need another player. You know, there's nothing like a good game of poker to wait out eternity." He pointed to an old chair parked in the shadows.

"Por favor, pull up a chair and sit a spell."

Don't Look Under the Bed

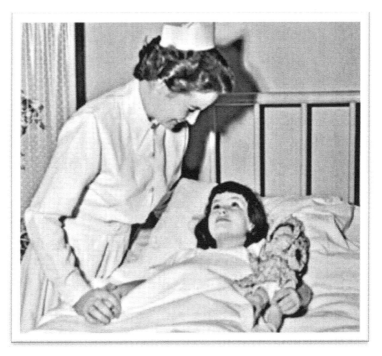

Chapter 12

Few people would ever believe that someone in the healthcare profession that swore on the nurse's oath would rather see children die than be healthy. But that is what happened at the United Verde Hospital in the 1920's.

Jerome's third hospital was built in 1917. Just one short year after the hospital opened, the rooms were overflowing with victims of the 1918 Spanish Influenza outbreak. They say that among those patients, there were at least 125 children from the Jerome area.

The operating room on the third floor witnessed many tragedies, including mining accidents, burns from the many fires and even shootings. Men lost arms, legs or were sometimes even blown apart from blasts in the underground mines. The patients who didn't make it were taken to the morgue located in the back of the building.

But with all these misfortunes, there was none as haunting as the suspicious deaths of approximately fifteen children at the United Verde Hospital. It happened over a four year period, from 1920 to 1924.

A pediatric nurse from Boston, Massachusetts named Margret Tilburg transferred to The United Verde Hospital in Jerome in 1920. She quickly worked her way to the position of Head Nurse. Nurse Tilburg always seemed to thrive on the excitement of an emergency. Strangely though, when a child was sick or injured and didn't make it, she never seemed affected at all by their death.

Rolando Flores was being treated for pneumonia, when suddenly he began having seizures and extensive, unexplained bleeding. Flores went into cardiac arrest and died while in the care of Nurse Tilburg.

Then, a six month old baby named Jose Santos also went into cardiac arrest. He was revived, but went into arrest again and during Tilburg's shift, the child died. The cause was unknown.

Another child, Mary Brown was sent to the pediatrics unit to recover from a routine surgery. She was progressing well and then, for no reason, became lethargic and started bleeding. Her condition continued to deteriorate and she soon died. Again, it was on Nurse Tilburg's shift.

It eventually became clear to everyone that children were dying in this unit from illnesses and injuries that should not have been fatal. It was also clear that these deaths always seemed to occur when Nurse Tilburg was present. Every one of the unexplained incidents happened on her shift and oddly, Nurse Tilburg would always insist on taking the corpse to the morgue herself.

"They're going to start thinking I'm the Death Nurse," Tilburg said one day.
In fact, some of the staff started calling her duty hours the "Death Shift".

One of the doctors suspected nurse Tilburg might have had a hand in the children's deaths, but he had no proof. The doctor was worried about bad publicity for the hospital and needed to find some answers quick, so he assigned a trusted intern to secretly follow her.

One afternoon the intern caught Nurse Tilburg injecting a liquid into a sick child's I.V. line with a large syringe, Tilburg, knowing she was caught red handed, squirted the fluid over the child in the sign of a cross. Then, with syringe in hand, she ran down the hallway and disappeared.

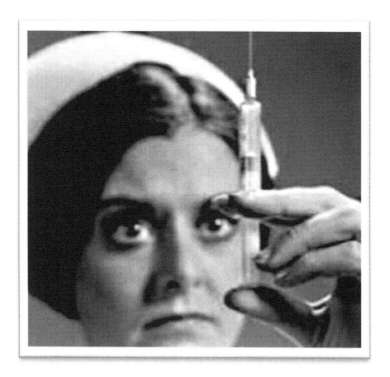

Of course, Nurse Tilburg did not show up for her shift the following day and no one had seen her since the incident. A few days later, a janitor found Nurse Margret Tilburg's dead body under a bed in a storage room. She had injected herself with the remainder of the solution and blood was everywhere. When the liquid in the syringe was tested, it was found to be a drug called *Heparin*, an anticoagulant.

The authorities then ordered several of the dead children exhumed and body tissues were tested. Their deaths appeared to have been caused by an overdose of heparin. Hospital records indicated that heparin had never been prescribed for any of these children. Soon, people began to gossip. The word was out and folks believed that Nurse Tilburg's evil spirit was now haunting the hospital. There was a local warning, that if your child had to be admitted into the hospital, under no circumstance should they be left alone.

Not only did this evil nurse severely compromise the hospital's reputation, but the building itself was also in danger. The hospital had been constructed on what is known as the "Verde Fault" and now, one end of the structure began to sink. The United Verde Copper Mining Company then soon made plans to build a fourth hospital.

Architects; Lescher and Mahoney of Phoenix gave out the details to the Verde Copper News;

Jerome; Tuesday, November 24, 1925;

The ground area will be 56 by 150 feet. The new hospital will be a beautiful building with three stories and a basement and a roof garden.

Elevator service will be maintained from the basement to the roof. Stairways will be of special composition tile. Four wards of eight beds, bringing the total capacity to 40 patients. The hospital will be concrete construction, an operating room, sterilizing room, X-ray room, kitchen, treatment room, physicians' offices, drug room and a morgue.

Construction on the new United Verde Hospital will begin this spring.

The new United Verde Hospital opened in January 27, 1927. The hospital became the most modern and well equipped hospital in Arizona and possibly in all of the western states.

The hospital operated for the next twenty-three years. When the mining operations closed in 1953, the hospital also closed its doors. The United Verde Hospital building stood unused and vacant for the next forty-four years.

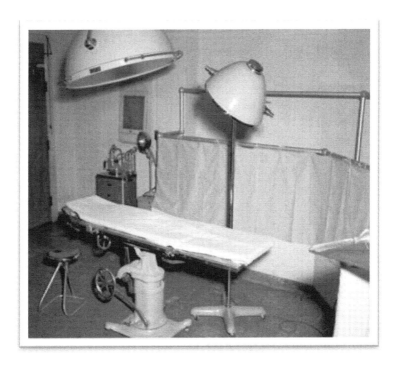

Many believed that during those years, the building was haunted.

The silhouette of a nurse in a white uniform and hat, presumably Nurse Tilburg had also been seen moving about the vacant corridors, occasionally peeking into rooms. Also, sounds of a hospital bed being raised and lowered and the squeaky wheels of a wheel chair rolling down the hallways were reported.

Today the United Verde Hospital is called The Jerome Grand Hotel and the Asylum Restaurant.

It currently provides 23 fully restored, modern rooms, a full service hotel with a bar, a restaurant, a gift shop and a 24-hour front desk.

Fortunately, Nurse Tilburg has not been seen since the hospital building became the popular and prestigious Jerome Grand Hotel. One would hope she has moved on to quieter surroundings.

When you turn out the lights and settle into bed, in those few seconds before you fall asleep, you might ask yourself this. Are you alone in the darkness? Or could Nurse Tilburg's ghost have returned? Whatever you decide, the best advice is, DON'T LOOK UNDER THE BED!

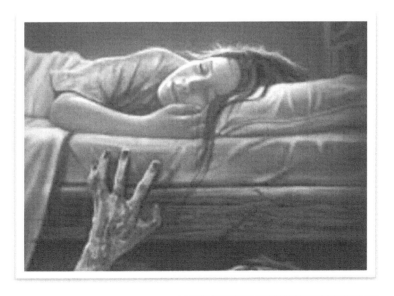

The Haunted Woods

Chapter 13

Rachel, soon to be fifteen was growing into a beautiful young woman. Her soft, dark eyes set off her shiny black hair. It was early spring and Rachel's Papa was planning her "Quinceañera" party. *(Quinceañera is the celebration of a girl's fifteenth birthday in Mexico and other parts of Latin America.)*

Rachel and her father lived in a small cabin at the edge of the woods in the Prescott National Forest. Rachel's Papa, as he was called did not have a lot of money, but would spend all he had for his only child.

Each day after school Rachel would sit on the back porch, strum her guitar and sing. Some say she had the voice of an Angel.

Hector was a local woodcutter and twice Rachel's age. One could always hear the sound of his axe on the hardwood trees, echoing through the forest. Every afternoon Hector would make it a practice to be in the vicinity of Rachel's home.

He would stop chopping wood, stand in the shadows and listen as Rachel sang. He was falling in love with Rachel; of course, she was unaware of his obsession.

The special day soon arrived and everyone in the town was invited. Rachel looked beautiful in her elegant full-length white dress, escorted by her proud Papa. The celebration would start at the Holy Catholic Church. After mass, they would proceed to a banquet hall for a festive dinner and dance reception.

Rachel danced with a handsome young man she knew from school named Manual.

Hector, the wood cutter stood quietly in the shadows watching them. Seeing Rachel and Manual together fueled a jealous rage inside him.

After the party, Manual asked Rachel's Papa if he could give her a ride home. Papa had known Manual's family for years and trusted the boy, so he consented as long as Rachel was home by ten.

Sadly, Rachel never made it home that night. Both Rachel and Manual vanished, seemingly without a trace.

Missing person flyers were posted all over town and several search parties were formed to look for the young couple. Hector, knowing the area, led a search party deep into the forest, but no trace of the missing couple was found. Some of the townsfolk thought the young couple may have simply slipped off and got married.

Weeks and months went by and the young couple's plight began to fade in the minds of the locals. Papa, of course, never forgot and was stricken with grief over his missing daughter.

The continuous chop, chop, chop was heard in the forest as Hector supplied everyone in the town with wood for the winter. Every afternoon around 3:00, however, the chopping sounds in the forest would stop. Rachel's Papa would stand on the back porch and listen.

Was his mind playing tricks on him, or was Rachel singing from the tree tops? As the weeks past, the singing became fainter and one day it stopped all together.

The leaves were almost gone from the trees and soon the long winter would set in.

It was a cold morning, just before dawn when a timid knock sounded upon the door of Rachel's Papa's home.

Looking through the window he saw a gaunt, ghostly figure on the porch. The figure was wearing a dirty, blood splattered, long white dress.

"Who's there?" Rachel's Papa said.

The ghostly figure only made a creepy airy sound. "Iyaaahaha."

Papa struck a match and tried to light his lantern, but his hands were shaking so much he couldn't get it lit. He looked to the window and a chill ran through his entire body. Staring back at him from the dark porch was a hideous, ghostly figure. There was matted hair hanging down in front of the creatures distorted face.

Who are you and what do you want?" Papa demanded.

The ghostly creature waved its hands, repeating the eerie sound. "Iyaaahaha.

Papa's voice cracked with fear as he grabbed his shotgun. "Go away or I'll shoot!

The ghostly figure pushed open the door and produced a bloody axe from beneath its tattered, clothes. Holding the ax in the air, the creature repeated, "Iyaaahaha".
Rachel's papa, now afraid for his life, fired his gun. The hideous creature fell backwards off the porch and lay on the ground. A crumpled piece of paper dropped from its hand. Papa waited until the creature stopped moving and carefully approached the corpse. He picked up the piece of paper and written in charcoal on the back of a missing person flyer was a note that read.

Dear Papa. If you are reading this note,
I made it home.I know that I'm no longer pretty,
but I love you very much.Hector, the wood cutter
kidnapped Manual and I that night after my
Quinceañera Party. He chopped Manual up
into little pieces and buried him beneath a
tall oak tree.I kept singing,I hoping you could
hear my voice and come rescue me,
but you never came. Hector got scared someone
would hear me so he cut my tongue out and
chopped my face up with his ax. I can no longer
speak or sing.This morning while Hector slept
I got myself untied grabbed his ax and hit him
in the head. I think he's dead, but I'm not sure.
I took his axe and climbed the tree.I've been
running all night to get home. Now I'm safe.
I love you Papa .
Your daughter Rachel.

Dear Papa, if you are reading this note I made it home. I know that I'm no longer pretty, but I love you very much.

Hector, the wood cutter kidnapped Manual and I that night after my Quinceañera Party. He chopped Manual up into little pieces and buried him beneath a tall oak tree and tied me up in his tree house. I kept singing, hoping you could hear my voice and come to rescue me, but you never came. Hector got scared someone would hear me so he cut my tongue out and chopped my face up with his ax. I can no longer speak or sing.

This morning while Hector slept I got myself untied grabbed his ax and hit him in the head. I think he's dead, but I'm not sure. I took his axe and climbed down the tree. I've been running all night to get home. Now I'm safe.
I love you Papa.
Your daughter Rachel.

After reading the note and realizing he had killed his only daughter, the anguish was too much for him to bear.

Distraught and sickened with grief, Rachel's papa carefully picked up his dead daughter and carried her inside. He laid her on a couch and covered her face with a sheet. Papa prayed over Rachel for a minute and then deliberately set the cabin ablaze, burning him, Rachel and the cabin to the ground.

At the top of Mingus Mountain, at the edge of the woods is a stone chimney where their cabin once stood.

Today, in a place the locals call "The Haunted Woods", you can still hear the sound of an axe on the hardwood trees as it echoes throughout the forest.

Then, everyday around 3:00, the forest goes silent. If you listen carefully, you can still hear the faint voice of an angel singing from the tree tops. You may even get a glimpse of a grieving, lonely, old man, wandering aimlessly where a small cabin once stood.